Genghis Khan

Hudson Murrell

Series Editor **Rob Waring**

Level 4 - ❽

Genghis Khan
Hudson Murrell

© 2017 Seed Learning, Inc.

Series Editor: Rob Waring
Acquisitions Editor: Liana Robinson
Copy Editor: Casey Malarcher
Cover/Interior Design: Andy Roh

ISBN: 978-1-9464-5239-9

10 9 8 7 6 5 4 3 2 1
21 20 19 18 17

Contents

Birth

Genghis Khan was one of the best known warriors and leaders of men that the world has ever known. He was born in about 1162. When he was born, his name was Temujin, and he was the son of a chief.

Genghis Khan

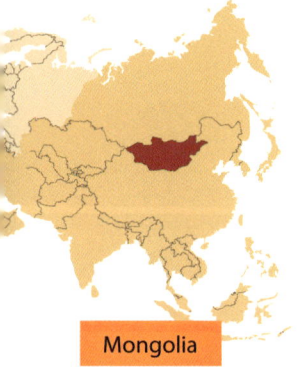

Mongolia

Stories say that Temujin was born with a blood clot in his hand. According to Mongolian folklore, this was a sign that he was destined to be a leader. His early years, however, made that seem unlikely.

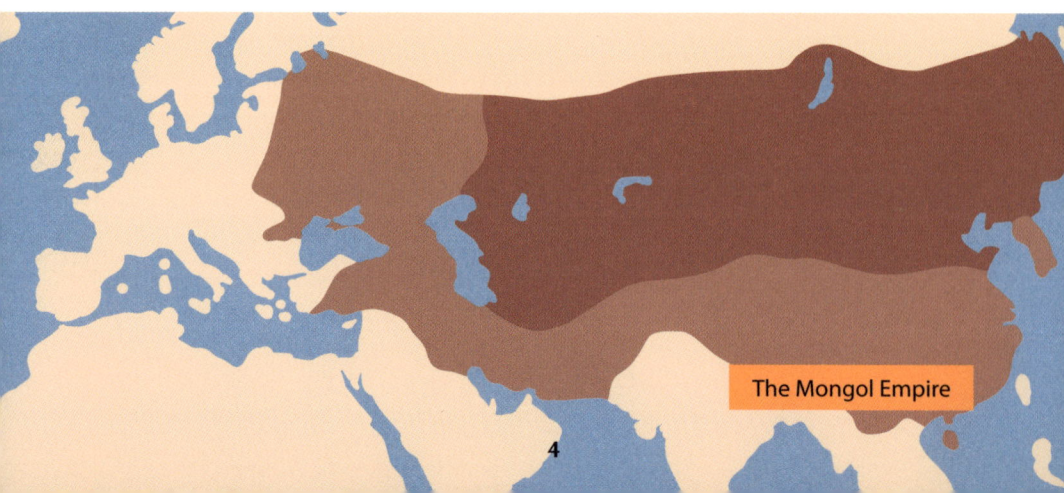

The Mongol Empire

A Hard Early Life

A rival killed his father when Temujin was only nine years old. After this, he and his family were left in extreme poverty. Their tribe abandoned them in the winter. Temujin and his family ate things like roots, wild fruit, and fish to survive. Temujin and his brothers had to work together. One brother tried to be independent and selfish, and he was killed.

Temujin grew in power and influence because of his fighting skills and also because of his will to fight hard. Temujin's enemies and rivals began to fear him.

At one point, a rival captured Temujin. One night, while his captors were eating, he escaped. This escape made his reputation grow even more.

Mongolian winter

Temujin hid in a river during his escape.

Growing into a Man

Even in happy times, there was violence in Temujin's life. He married early, but his wife was captured by a rival clan. He was very angry and thought of a plan to get her back. However, he needed help in order to do this.

Another clan leader saw Temujin's strength, and they became friends. Together, they gathered warriors and defeated those who took his wife.

Genghis would become the most famous Mongolian ever.

Temujin Becomes a Leader

Temujin's success in life was mostly due to his skills on horseback, with a bow and arrow, and in wrestling. His success attracted more and more warriors to join him.

The bows the Mongol warriors used were very strong.

After each victory, he took the land from the people he defeated. He soon became a clan leader. The common people he defeated had a simple choice—join him or die.

Mongol warriors were experts with bows and arrows, even while racing on horseback.

Temujin Becomes Genghis Khan

All of the Mongol clans declared Temujin to be their leader in the beginning of the 13th century. They gave him the title "Genghis Khan" which can be translated as "universal ruler." As the leader of the clans, Genghis Khan wanted to help the people. He wanted to make them feel a sense of community. Therefore, he made a code called "yasa" to guide people in their daily lives.

It is said that Genghis had a large personal guard. He was well-protected. He also had an extensive spy network.

"Khan" means leader.

The Start of His Empire

Genghis fought many violent battles to get more land. He fought and won anywhere, in flatlands, hills, or mountains. One of Genghis's enemies was the Jin people. The Jin controlled China, with an emperor and strong military leaders.

Genghis was always fighting in northern China, taking land and people when he won. One famous battle against the Jin happened in 1211 in the mountains at Badger Mouth Pass near modern-day Beijing. In this battle, Genghis had less than 100,000 warriors while the Jin had at least 300,000 warriors.

Mountains near Badger Mouth Pass

The Battle of Badger Mouth Pass

The two armies met at a place that favored the Mongols. Behind the Jin army was a narrow bottleneck. And because of the way they had been marching, the Jin army had its cavalry in front and infantry at the back. Genghis and his generals saw this and attacked at once.

The Mongols attacked

The Jin cavalry was driven back, but they did not have enough room because of the bottleneck. The retreating cavalry got in the way of the infantry and caused confusion. A great number of Jin soldiers were killed.

Steep mountain cliffs created a bottleneck.

Statues of the warriors of Genghis Khan

The leader of the Jins, Wanyan Yongji, and his remaining soldiers escaped to Huihe Fortress. They were surrounded and attacked by the Mongols. The Jin army was destroyed, but Wanyan Yongji escaped. He fled to Zhongdu (modern-day Beijing). So Genghis led his army south toward the walled city of Beijing.

The Attack on Beijing

Before Genghis arrived, Wanyan Yongji was killed. The new leader acknowledged Genghis Khan as his overlord and gave him valuable gifts such as gold and silver in order to save the city from attack. Genghis happily took these gifts and went home.

It did not take the new leader long to anger Genghis, and in 1215, the Mongol leader marched back to Beijing. The large city had a wall with 1,000 guard towers around it. It was too tall to attack, so Genghis decided that the Jin should not get out.

Parts of the wall in Beijing still exist today.

Mongolian warriors heading toward Beijing

Burning farmland

Genghis burned the area outside the wall. His men then surrounded the wall, so no food could get into the city.

Genghis's plan worked. Beijing didn't have enough food, so the Jin gave up. Genghis allowed his soldiers to sack the city. His soldiers devastated the city and made off with all the treasure. As for Genghis Khan, he went back to Mongolia.

The Jin surrendered Beijing.

Speed Wins Battles

From his early days as a clan leader, Genghis practiced for battle. One way that he practiced was to train his horses daily. His horses could run very long distances quickly, so he was always ready for battle.

Genghis's army could suddenly appear and attack quickly. After victories, Genghis would move on to get new lands. However, the defeated people always feared his quick return.

Mongolian horses were bred for strength and speed.

The traditional house, a ger, was easy to put up and take down. This is a modern-day ger in Mongolia.

14

Expanding the Empire

The Mongolians in battle

Genghis's empire now touched the Khwarezm Empire. Genghis wanted to trade with this empire, so he sent gifts and merchants to Muhammad, their leader. The governor of the city of Utrar, in present-day Kazakhstan, made a huge mistake. He captured and killed Genghis's people.

Genghis, angered, sent an ambassador to demand that the governor be handed over. Muhammad killed the ambassador and sent his head back to Genghis.

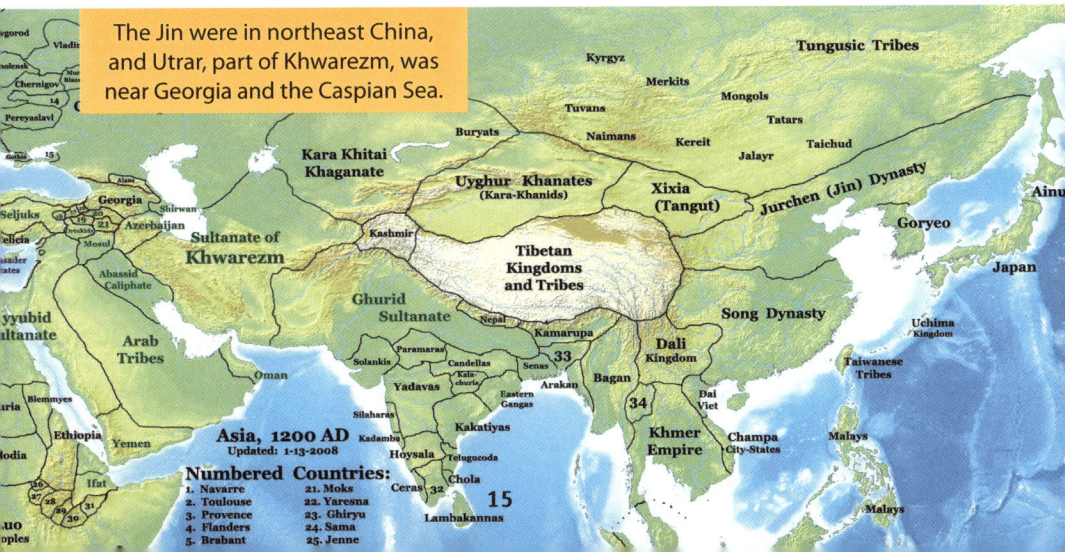

The Jin were in northeast China, and Utrar, part of Khwarezm, was near Georgia and the Caspian Sea.

Asia, 1200 AD
Updated: 1-13-2008

Numbered Countries:
1. Navarre   21. Moks
2. Toulouse   22. Yaresna
3. Provence   23. Ghiryu
4. Flanders   24. Sama
5. Brabant   25. Jenne

15

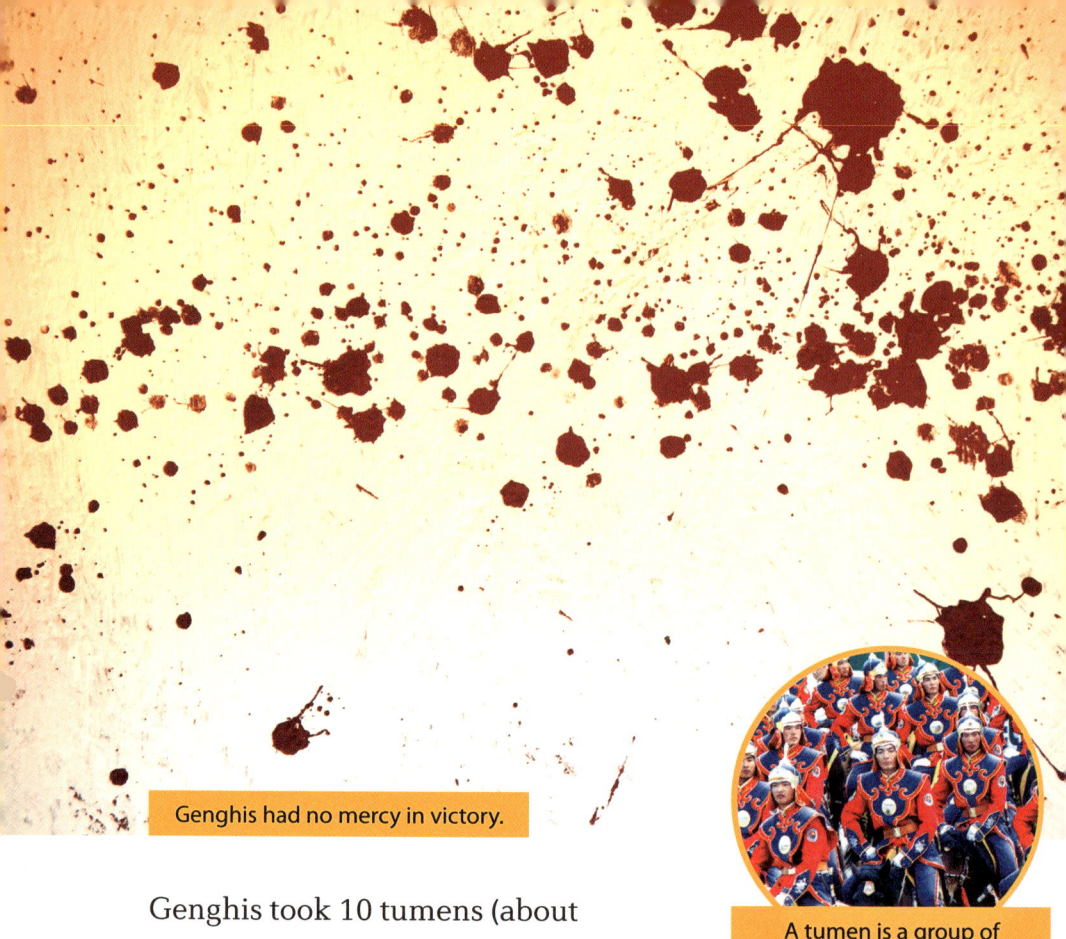

Genghis had no mercy in victory.

A tumen is a group of 10,000 warriors. Ten tumens is 100,000 warriors.

Genghis took 10 tumens (about 100,000 men) with him to fight in Utrar. Muhammad had around 400,000 soldiers, so he probably was not worried.

Genghis split his army and surrounded Muhammad and his troops. Muhammad held out for about a month, but Genghis and his men were victorious.

His revenge was brutal. Whole cities were destroyed—including the people.

Genghis the Legend

Genghis Khan conquered parts of Afghanistan and Russia as well. The battles were bloody, and the number of deaths was high. The Mongols took a huge amount of wealth from Central Asia.

Even his death in 1227 did not stop Genghis. The need to conquer and get more land was passed on to his sons and grandsons. Genghis Khan was the most feared leader that Asia has ever known.

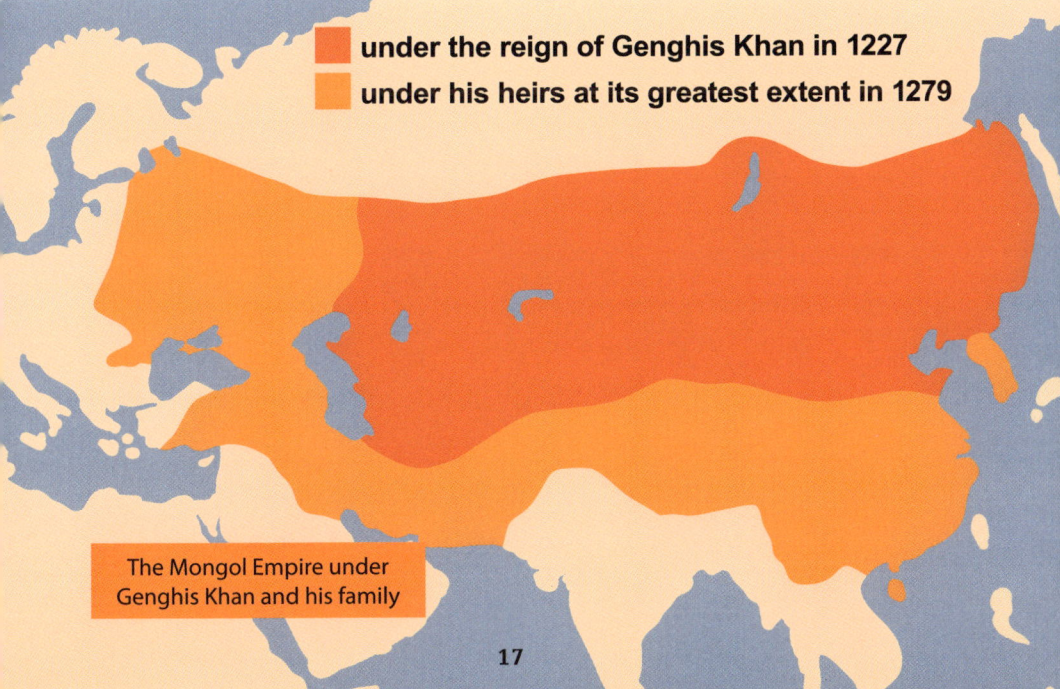

under the reign of Genghis Khan in 1227
under his heirs at its greatest extent in 1279

The Mongol Empire under Genghis Khan and his family

Comprehension Questions

1. What was an early sign that Genghis Khan would be a leader?
   - (a) Cuts on his face
   - (b) A blood clot in his hand
   - (c) The death of his mother
   - (d) The death of his father

2. During his early life, Temujin became popular because…
   - (a) he was a great fighter.
   - (b) he was a great speaker.
   - (c) his father was the king.
   - (d) he was a good horse rider.

3. What happened to Temujin's wife?
   - (a) She became a clan leader.
   - (b) She fell off a horse.
   - (c) She was taken.
   - (d) She became a warrior.

4. What is NOT one of the three skills Mongolian warriors must be good at?
   - (a) Horse riding
   - (b) Wrestling
   - (c) Shooting arrows
   - (d) Sword fighting

5. To unite people, Genghis created a "yasa" which instructed people on…
   - (a) how to fight.
   - (b) how to build cities.
   - (c) how to live.
   - (d) how to study.

6. The Mongols were often…
   - (a) outnumbered in battle.
   - (b) feared.
   - (c) fighting to get more land.
   - (d) All of the above

7. When Genghis defeated his enemies, he told the common people to…
   - (a) leave quickly.
   - (b) feed his soldiers.
   - (c) quit fighting.
   - (d) join him or die.

8. Muhammad angered Genghis by…
   - (a) killing his merchants.
   - (b) not handing over the governor.
   - (c) killing his ambassador.
   - (d) All of the above

9. Genghis is famous now because he…
   - (a) built a great and beautiful city.
   - (b) conquered large areas and killed many people.
   - (c) created the "yasa."
   - (d) defeated the Jin at Utrar.

10. What happened when Genghis died?
    - (a) All the battles stopped.
    - (b) His family continued to fight.
    - (c) His country collapsed.
    - (d) All his family members were killed.

Glossary

- **abandon** to leave someone or something without any intention to return to it

- **ambassador** a person who officially represents his or her country in a different country

- **blood clot** a thick mass of blood

- **bottleneck** a place where a road or passage becomes narrow which causes those using the road to slow down or stop

- **cavalry** a group of soldiers in an army who fight on horses

- **clan** a group of people living together with one leader

- **conquer** to gain victory, especially in battle

- **governor** a person in charge of a region

- **merchant** a person who buys and sells goods

- **Mongolia** a country in Asia between China and Russia

- **poverty** the state of being very poor

- **rival** a person competing with others for the same thing

- **surrender** to stop fighting and give oneself up to another

- **tumen** a group of 10,000 Mongolian soldiers

- **warrior** a person who fights in battles and is known for having experience and skill

Image Credit/Pages

World History
Timeline

This chart shows a rough overview of world history.
Some of the dates have been simplified.

World History Timeline

	2900 BC	2800 BC	2700 BC	2600 BC	2500 BC

Narmer, Egyptian King
(c. 3000 BC)

Pyramids of Giza
(built c. 2550-2490 BC)

Cuneiform (c. 3000 BC-100 AD)

Old Egyptian Kingdom (c. 2686 BC)

	2900 BC	2800 BC	2700 BC	2600 BC	2500 BC

⟵ 5000 BC Mesopotamia (Sumerians)

⟵ 3100 BC Early Dynastic Period of Egypt   Old Egyptian Kingdom

⟵ 3650 BC Minoan Civilization (Crete)

Early Bronze Age

	2900 BC	2800 BC	2700 BC	2600 BC	2500 BC

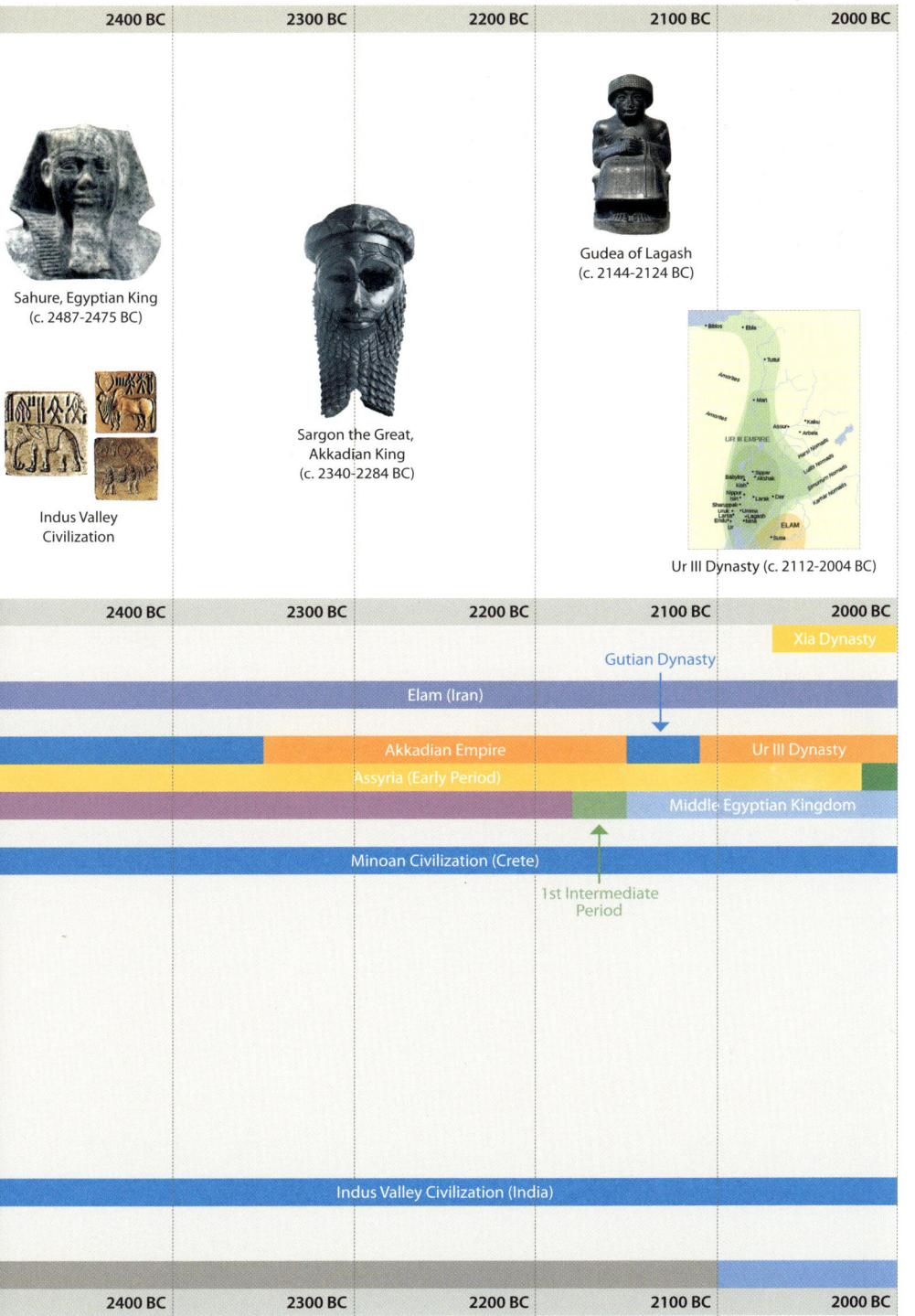

| 2400 BC | 2300 BC | 2200 BC | 2100 BC | 2000 BC |

Sahure, Egyptian King
(c. 2487-2475 BC)

Indus Valley
Civilization

Sargon the Great,
Akkadian King
(c. 2340-2284 BC)

Gudea of Lagash
(c. 2144-2124 BC)

Ur III Dynasty (c. 2112-2004 BC)

| 2400 BC | 2300 BC | 2200 BC | 2100 BC | 2000 BC |

Xia Dynasty

Gutian Dynasty

Elam (Iran)

Akkadian Empire

Ur III Dynasty

Assyria (Early Period)

Middle Egyptian Kingdom

Minoan Civilization (Crete)

1st Intermediate
Period

Indus Valley Civilization (India)

| 2400 BC | 2300 BC | 2200 BC | 2100 BC | 2000 BC |

World History Timeline

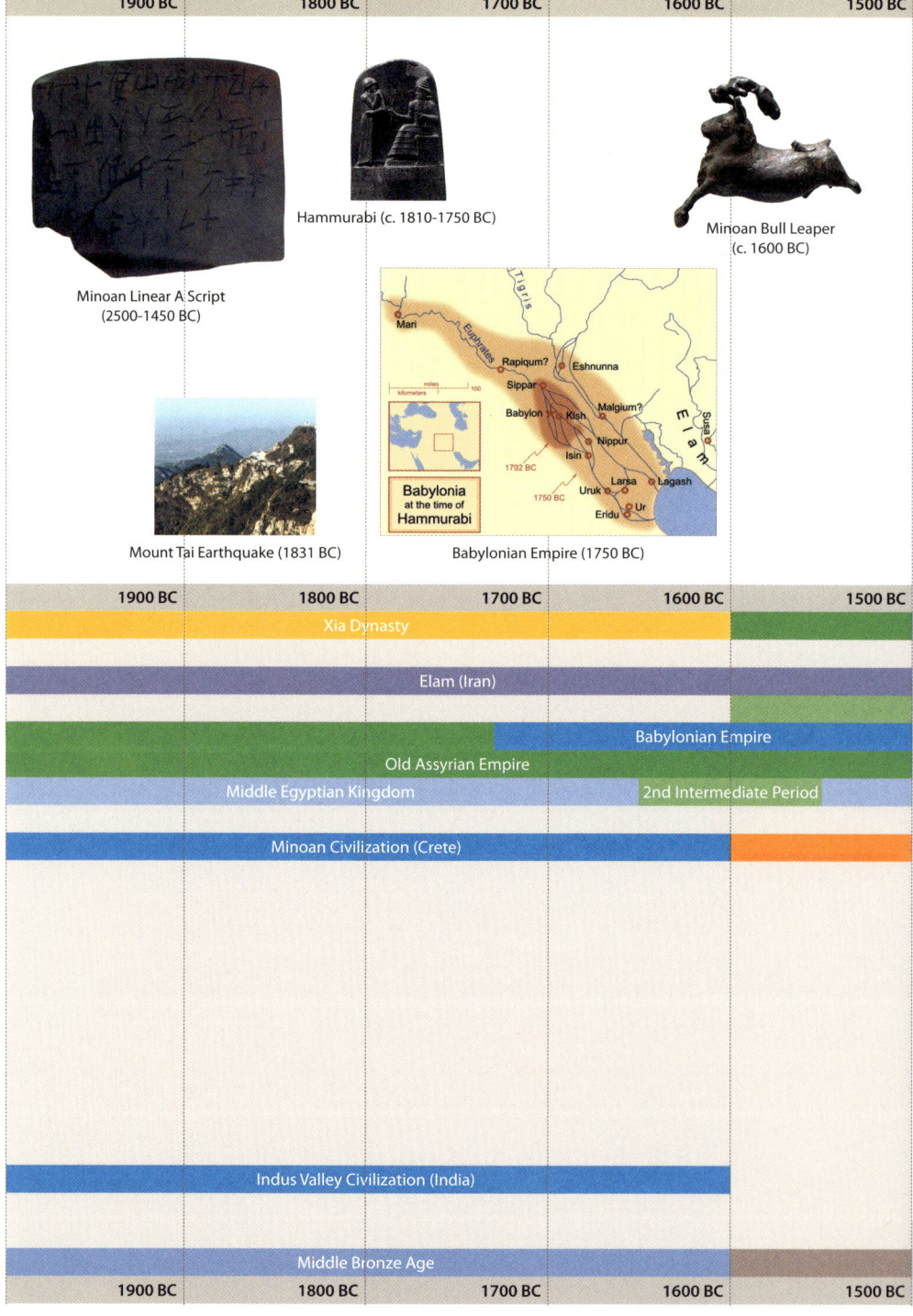

1900 BC	1800 BC	1700 BC	1600 BC	1500 BC

Minoan Linear A Script
(2500-1450 BC)

Hammurabi (c. 1810-1750 BC)

Minoan Bull Leaper
(c. 1600 BC)

Mount Tai Earthquake (1831 BC)

Babylonia
at the time of
Hammurabi

Babylonian Empire (1750 BC)

1900 BC	1800 BC	1700 BC	1600 BC	1500 BC

Xia Dynasty

Elam (Iran)

Babylonian Empire

Old Assyrian Empire

Middle Egyptian Kingdom

2nd Intermediate Period

Minoan Civilization (Crete)

Indus Valley Civilization (India)

Middle Bronze Age

1900 BC	1800 BC	1700 BC	1600 BC	1500 BC

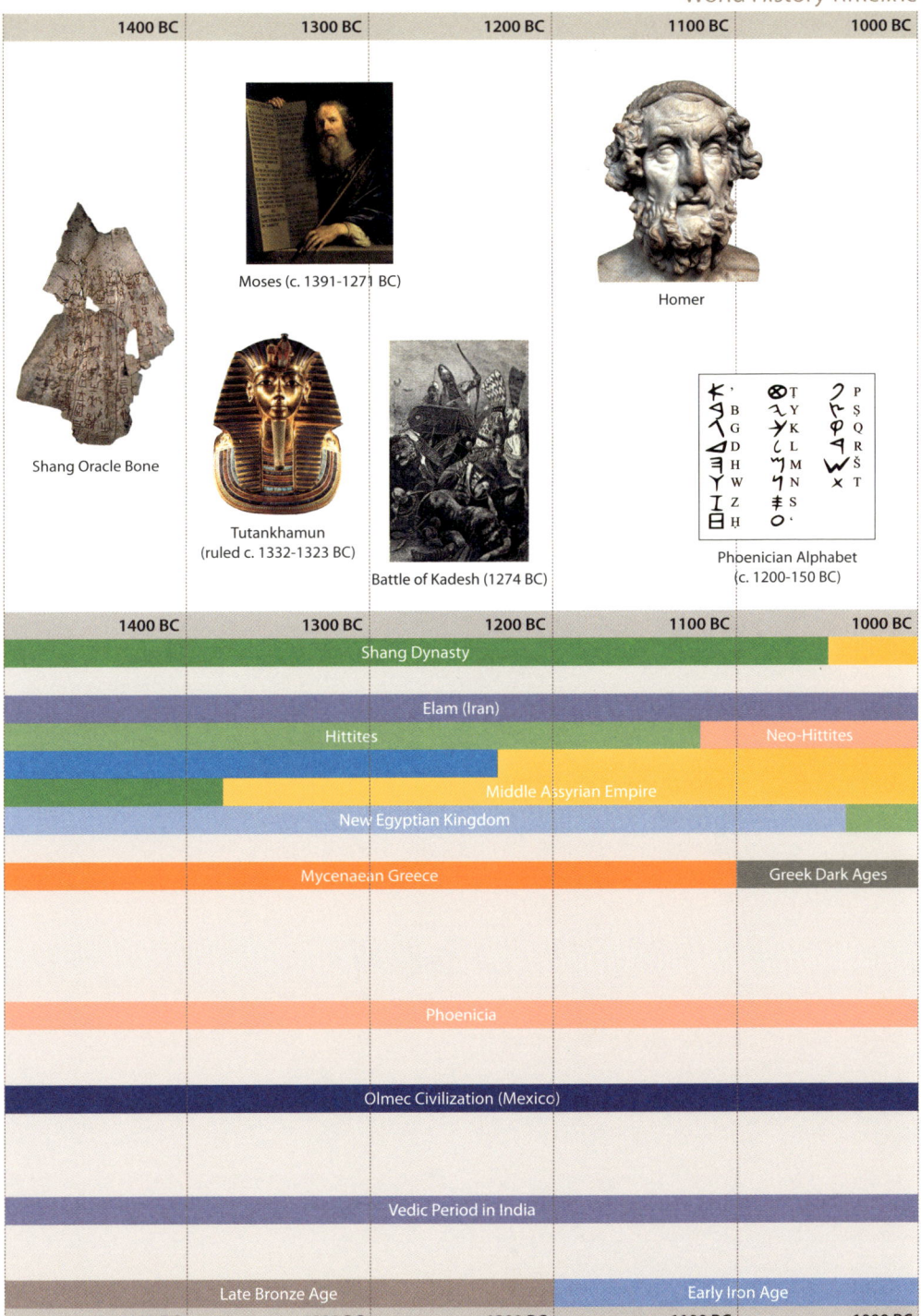

| 1400 BC | 1300 BC | 1200 BC | 1100 BC | 1000 BC |

Moses (c. 1391-1271 BC)

Homer

Shang Oracle Bone

Tutankhamun
(ruled c. 1332-1323 BC)

Battle of Kadesh (1274 BC)

Phoenician Alphabet
(c. 1200-150 BC)

| 1400 BC | 1300 BC | 1200 BC | 1100 BC | 1000 BC |

Shang Dynasty

Elam (Iran)

Hittites

Neo-Hittites

Middle Assyrian Empire

New Egyptian Kingdom

Mycenaean Greece

Greek Dark Ages

Phoenicia

Olmec Civilization (Mexico)

Vedic Period in India

Late Bronze Age

Early Iron Age

| 1400 BC | 1300 BC | 1200 BC | 1100 BC | 1000 BC |

World History Timeline

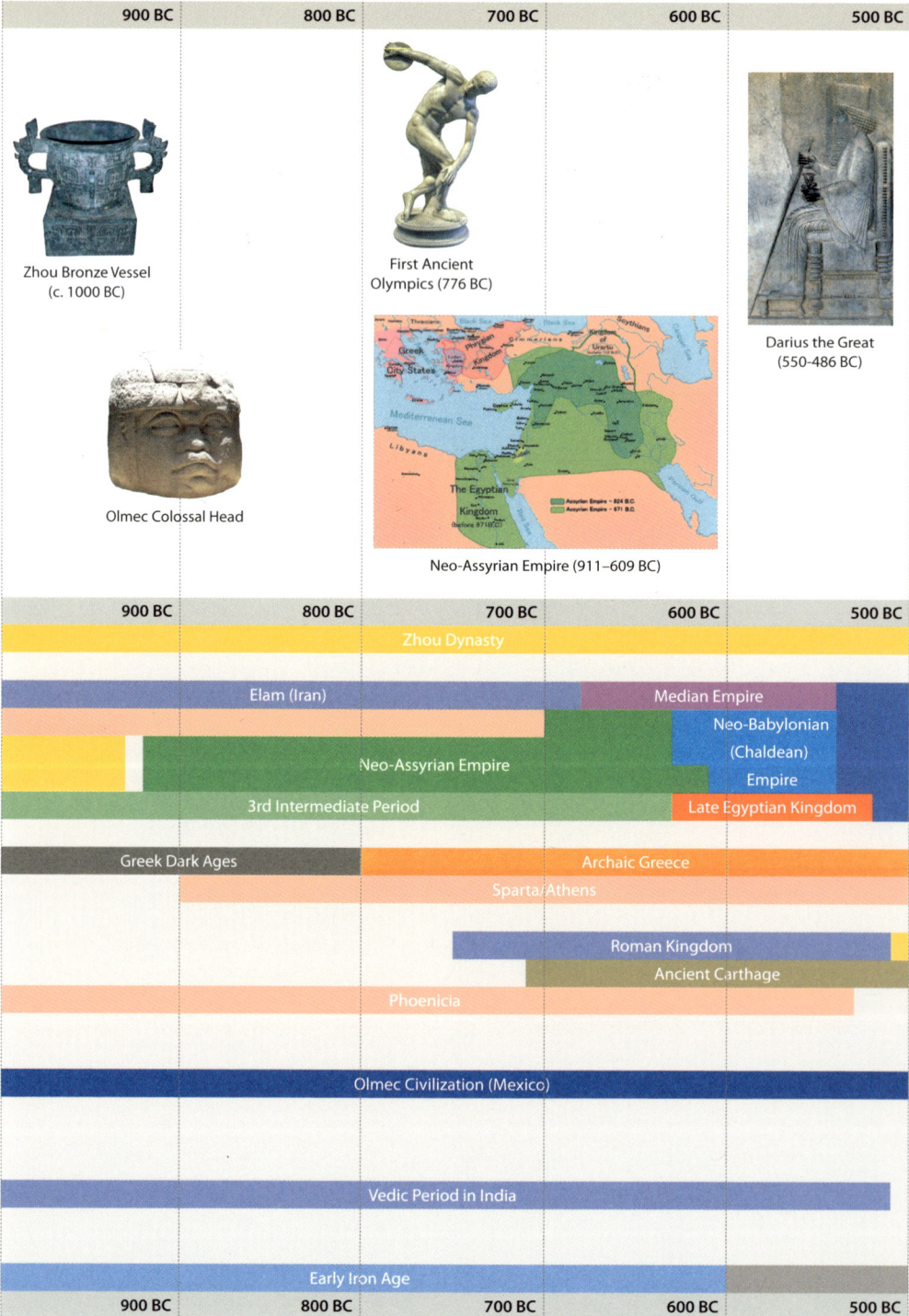

| 900 BC | 800 BC | 700 BC | 600 BC | 500 BC |

Zhou Bronze Vessel
(c. 1000 BC)

First Ancient
Olympics (776 BC)

Darius the Great
(550–486 BC)

Olmec Colossal Head

Neo-Assyrian Empire (911–609 BC)

| 900 BC | 800 BC | 700 BC | 600 BC | 500 BC |

Zhou Dynasty

Elam (Iran)

Median Empire

Neo-Babylonian (Chaldean) Empire

Neo-Assyrian Empire

3rd Intermediate Period

Late Egyptian Kingdom

Greek Dark Ages

Archaic Greece

Sparta/Athens

Roman Kingdom

Ancient Carthage

Phoenicia

Olmec Civilization (Mexico)

Vedic Period in India

Early Iron Age

| 900 BC | 800 BC | 700 BC | 600 BC | 500 BC |

World History Timeline

| 400 BC | 300 BC | 200 BC | 100 BC | 0 |

Alexander the Great
(356-323 BC)

Hannibal
(247-183 BC)

Julius Caesar
(100-44 BC)

Cleopatra
(69-30 BC)

Battle of Salamis
(480 BC)

Seleucid Empire (312-63 BC)

Rossetta Stone
(created 196 BC)

| 400 BC | 300 BC | 200 BC | 100 BC | 0 |

Zhou Dynasty

Qin

Han Dynasty

Achaemenid (Persian) Empire

Alexander the Great

Parthian Empire

Seleucid Empire
Ptolemaic Kingdom
(Hellenistic Greece)

Classical Greece

Sparta/Athens

Roman Empire

Roman Republic

Roman Empire

Maurya Empire

Middle Iron Age

| 400 BC | 300 BC | 200 BC | 100 BC | 0 |

World History Timeline

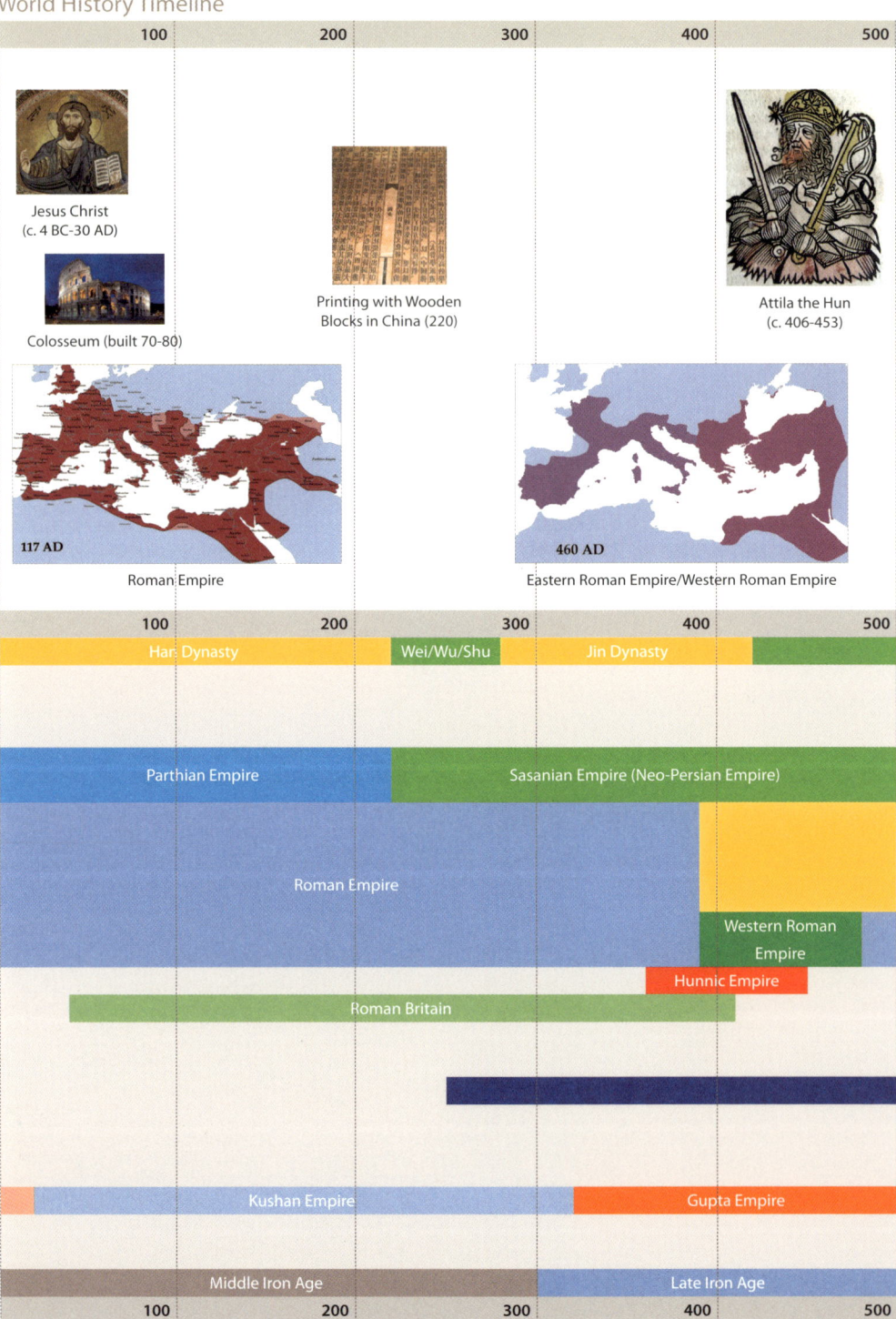

| | 100 | 200 | 300 | 400 | 500 |

Jesus Christ
(c. 4 BC-30 AD)

Colosseum (built 70-80)

Printing with Wooden
Blocks in China (220)

Attila the Hun
(c. 406-453)

117 AD
Roman Empire

460 AD
Eastern Roman Empire/Western Roman Empire

| 100 | 200 | 300 | 400 | 500 |

Han Dynasty

Wei/Wu/Shu

Jin Dynasty

Parthian Empire

Sasanian Empire (Neo-Persian Empire)

Roman Empire

Western Roman Empire

Hunnic Empire

Roman Britain

Kushan Empire

Gupta Empire

Middle Iron Age

Late Iron Age

| 100 | 200 | 300 | 400 | 500 |

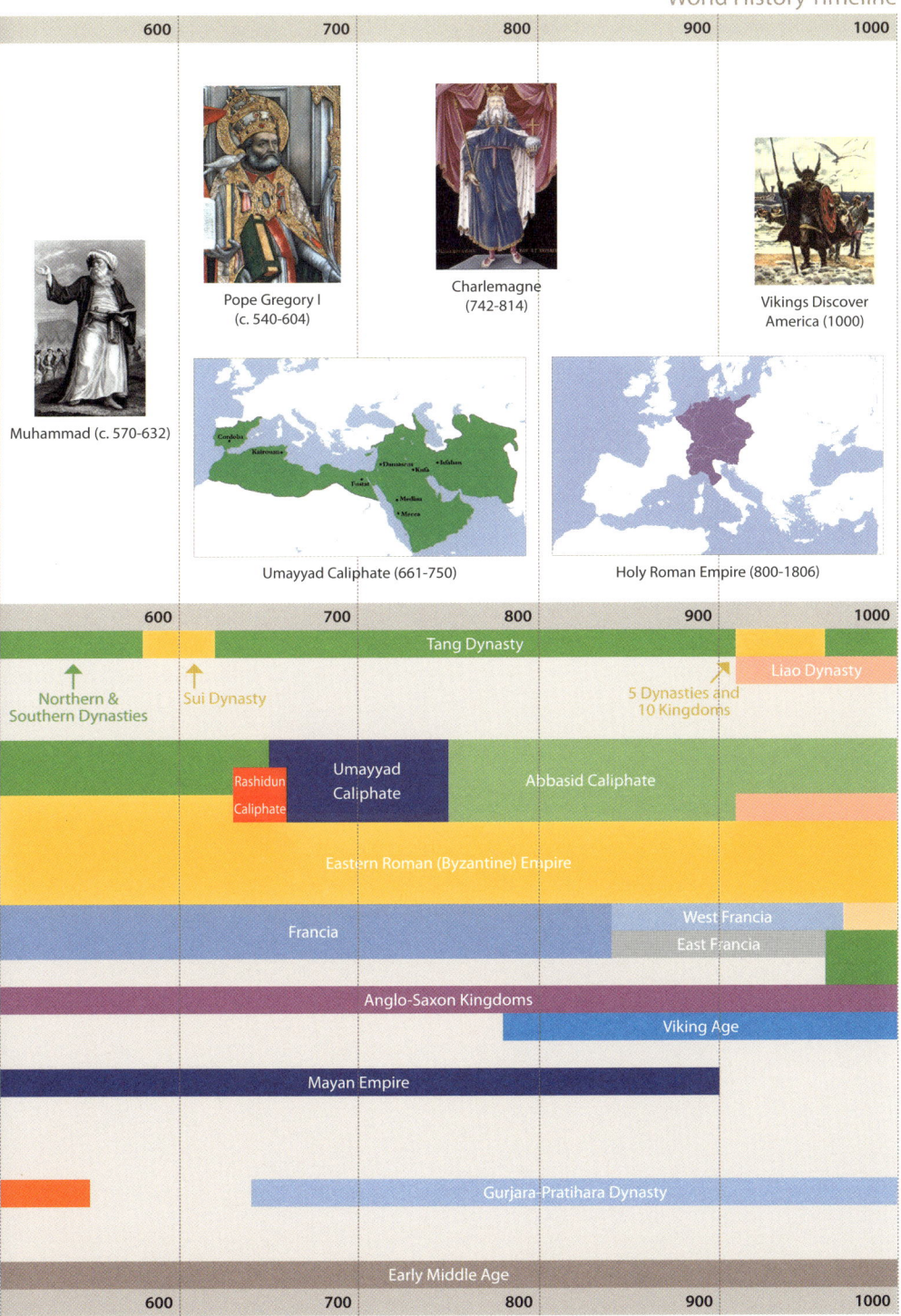

Muhammad (c. 570-632)

Pope Gregory I
(c. 540-604)

Charlemagne
(742-814)

Vikings Discover
America (1000)

Umayyad Caliphate (661-750)

Holy Roman Empire (800-1806)

| 600 | 700 | 800 | 900 | 1000 |

Tang Dynasty

Liao Dynasty

Northern &
Southern Dynasties

Sui Dynasty

5 Dynasties and
10 Kingdoms

Rashidun
Caliphate

Umayyad
Caliphate

Abbasid Caliphate

Eastern Roman (Byzantine) Empire

Francia

West Francia

East Francia

Anglo-Saxon Kingdoms

Viking Age

Mayan Empire

Gurjara-Pratihara Dynasty

Early Middle Age

| 600 | 700 | 800 | 900 | 1000 |

World History Timeline

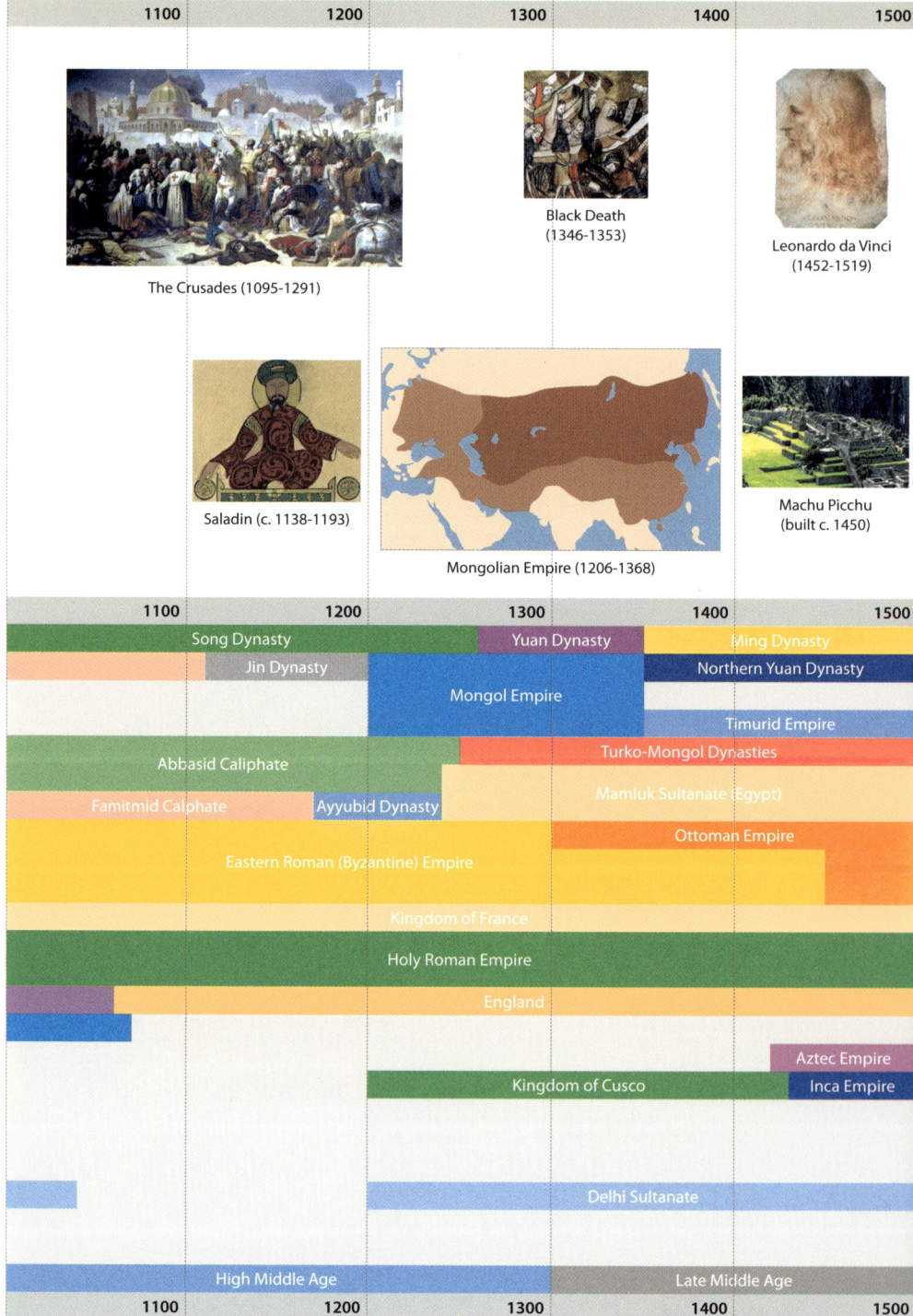

The Crusades (1095-1291)

Black Death (1346-1353)

Leonardo da Vinci (1452-1519)

Saladin (c. 1138-1193)

Mongolian Empire (1206-1368)

Machu Picchu (built c. 1450)

| 1100 | 1200 | 1300 | 1400 | 1500 |

Song Dynasty

Yuan Dynasty

Ming Dynasty

Jin Dynasty

Northern Yuan Dynasty

Mongol Empire

Timurid Empire

Abbasid Caliphate

Turko-Mongol Dynasties

Famitmid Caliphate

Ayyubid Dynasty

Mamluk Sultanate (Egypt)

Ottoman Empire

Eastern Roman (Byzantine) Empire

Kingdom of France

Holy Roman Empire

England

Aztec Empire

Kingdom of Cusco

Inca Empire

Delhi Sultanate

High Middle Age

Late Middle Age

| 1100 | 1200 | 1300 | 1400 | 1500 |

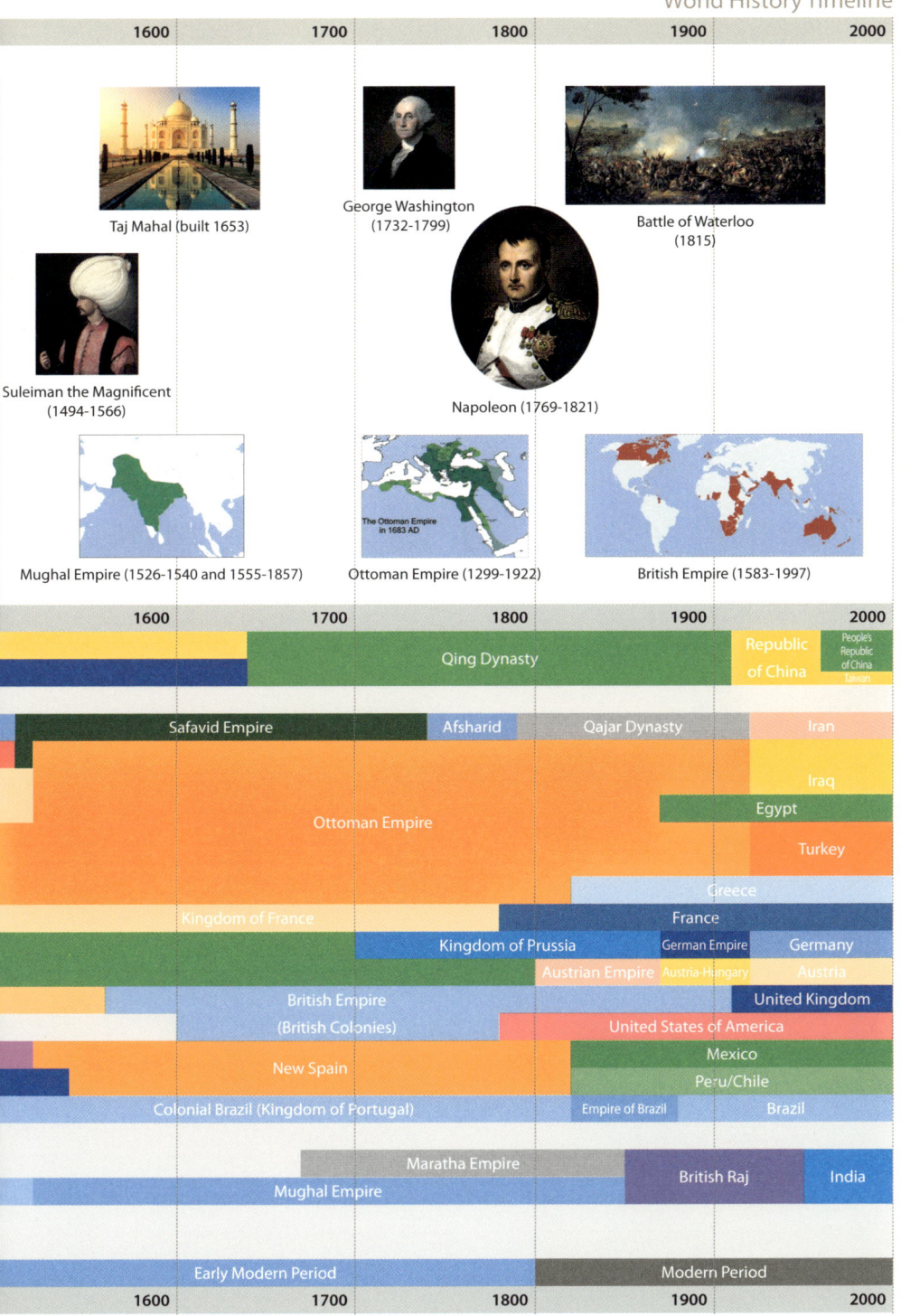

| 1600 | 1700 | 1800 | 1900 | 2000 |

Taj Mahal (built 1653)

George Washington
(1732-1799)

Battle of Waterloo
(1815)

Suleiman the Magnificent
(1494-1566)

Napoleon (1769-1821)

The Ottoman Empire
in 1683 AD

Mughal Empire (1526-1540 and 1555-1857)

Ottoman Empire (1299-1922)

British Empire (1583-1997)

| 1600 | 1700 | 1800 | 1900 | 2000 |

Qing Dynasty

Republic of China

People's Republic of China

Taiwan

Safavid Empire

Afsharid

Qajar Dynasty

Iran

Iraq

Ottoman Empire

Egypt

Turkey

Greece

Kingdom of France

France

Kingdom of Prussia

German Empire

Germany

Austrian Empire

Austria-Hungary

Austria

British Empire

United Kingdom

(British Colonies)

United States of America

New Spain

Mexico

Peru/Chile

Colonial Brazil (Kingdom of Portugal)

Empire of Brazil

Brazil

Maratha Empire

British Raj

India

Mughal Empire

Early Modern Period

Modern Period

| 1600 | 1700 | 1800 | 1900 | 2000 |

List of Books